Basic Quiltmaking Techniques

for Hand Appliqué

Mimi Dietrich

That Patchwork Place®

An Imprint of
Martingale & Company

Credits

Editor-in-Chief .... Kerry I. Smith
Technical Editors .... Barbara Weiland, Ursula Reikes
Managing Editor ....Judy Petry
Design Director....................................... Cheryl Stevenson
Cover Designer .... Margrit Baurecht
Text Designer .... Laurel Strand
Production Assistant .... Marijane E. Figg
Copy Editor ....Liz McGehee
Proofreader .... Kathleen Pike
Illustrator .... Robin Strobel
Photographer .... Brent Kane

Basic Quiltmaking Techniques for Hand Appliqué
© 1998 by Mimi Dietrich

& C O M P A N Y

Martingale & Company
PO Box 118
Bothell, WA 98041-0118 USA

Printed in Canada
03 02 01 00 99 98   6 5 4 3 2 1

Library of Congress Cataloging-in-Publication Data

Dietrich, Mimi.
    Basic quiltmaking techniques for hand appliqué/Mimi Dietrich.
        p. cm.
    Includes bibliographical references (p.).
    ISBN 1-56477-220-9
    1. Appliqué—Patterns. 2. Patchwork—Patterns. 3. Quilting—Patterns. I. Title.
TT779.D542 1998
746.46'041—dc21   98-4669
                                                                    CIP

Dedication

Kaitlin Scott is a young quilter who helped me sew one of the quilts and prepare many of the appliqué pieces. Kaitlin represents the future of quilting. This book is dedicated to her!

Acknowledgments

Many thanks to the special people who supported me throughout the writing of this book:

The editorial team at That Patchwork Place, who are always encouraging and supportive of my quilting projects;

Carol Doak, author of *Your First Quilt Book (or it should be!)*, who jump-started this project on a fun trip to Baltimore;

Monday Night Madness Quilters, who were invaluable in helping me finish the quilts on time: Phyllis Hess, Laurie Scott, Joan Costello, Barbara McMahon, Sue Brunt, and Vivian Schafer;

Norma Campbell, who quilted the table runner and always brings enthusiasm to the world of quilting;

Laurie Scott, who sent Kaitlin to me for a week;

The staff at Seminole Sampler Quilt Shop, who are very patient when searching for the "perfect" fabrics, especially Robbyn, Libbie, Helen, Susan, Arlene, and Marty;

And especially to Bob, Jon, and Ryan Dietrich, who provide computer assistance, patience, love, and fast food on busy days!

MISSION STATEMENT

WE ARE DEDICATED TO PROVIDING QUALITY PRODUCTS AND SERVICE BY WORKING TOGETHER TO INSPIRE CREATIVITY AND TO ENRICH THE LIVES WE TOUCH.

14.95

Table of Contents

Foreword 4

Preface 5

Introduction 6

Appliqué Terms 7

Fabric Selection 7

Background Fabrics 7

Appliqué Fabrics 8

Fabric Grain 9

Fabric Paste-Ups 9

Fabric Preparation 10

Tools and Supplies 10

Getting Ready to Hand Appliqué 12

Cutting Background Squares 12

Marking Appliqué Placement 12

Making Appliqué Templates 13

Preparation Techniques for Sure Success 13

Thread Basting Preparation 13

Gluestick Preparation 15

Starch Preparation 16

Curve and Point Preparation 17

Outside Curves 17

Inside Curves 17

Outside Points 18

Inside Points 18

Getting Ready to Sew 19

Pin Basting 19

Glue Basting 19

Hand Basting 19

Stitching Appliqués in Place 20

Threading the Needle and Tying a Knot 20

The Traditional Appliqué Stitch 20

Stitching Secrets 22

Straight Edges 22

Curves 22

Outside Points 22

Inside Points 22

Stems 23

Perfect Circles 24

Layered Appliqué 25

Needle-Turn Appliqué 26

Finishing Touches 27

Removing the Freezer Paper 27

Washing and Pressing Your Finished Blocks 27

Quilting 27

Signing Your Quilt 28

Projects 29

Spring Basket Pillow 29

Rosies and Posies Table Runner 35

Wall Quilts 40

School's Out 40

Dutch Treat 44

A Dozen Red Roses 57

Variation: Rainbow Roses 60

Welcome 62

Starlight, Starbright 66

Songs for All Seasons 70

Gallery 49

Suggested Books 79

Mail-Order Shopping 79

About the Author 80

Foreword

Basic Quiltmaking Techniques for Hand Appliqué is our first book in the Basic Quiltmaking Techniques series. This series is designed to take you beyond the foundations of basic quiltmaking you learned in *Your First Quilt Book (or it should be!)* and to expand your horizons with additional techniques for even more fun and creativity. Inside, you will find the same conversational style and easy learning approach that you found in *Your First Quilt Book (or it should be!)*.

Hand appliqué will expand your quiltmaking skills and offers you the opportunity to incorporate this technique into your quiltmaking projects. The basic quiltmaking information provided in *Your First Quilt Book (or it should be!)* will not be repeated in this book so you can focus on this new information.

With appliqué being her first love and specialty, Mimi Dietrich is the perfect person to introduce you to this new skill. In this book, she shares hand-appliqué techniques that are sure to prove successful for beginners. She has created a wonderful group of appliqué designs just for you—designs you can use to practice your new skills while you create wonderful keepsakes.

I am confident you will enjoy learning about hand appliqué with Mimi as you work on these delightful projects.

Carol Doak

Preface

I love appliqué! For me, there's something magical about choosing and hand stitching colorful fabrics to create pretty designs on larger fabric squares. I made my first quilt for my first child more than twenty years ago. Of course, it was an appliquéd quilt! Since that first quilt, I've made patchwork quilts of all kinds—Nine Patches, stars, flowers, Irish Chains, Log Cabins—but my favorite quilts are always the appliquéd ones.

It's fun to choose fabrics that are perfect for the appliquéd shapes and watch the designs come alive with color. I can stitch flowers that last a long time (and don't need watering)! There's a wonderful freedom in appliqué—flowers and leaves can sway in the wind, and fish can swim backwards in the water if I want them to. Best of all, I don't have to worry about cutting off patchwork points! Appliqué designs do not have to fit precisely together like puzzle pieces. A small variation in an appliqué design will not affect the whole piece.

Hand appliqué is a very portable method of quilting. You can prepare your project pieces and organize them in a small plastic bag so you can take them wherever you go. That way, they are there with you whenever you find yourself with a few extra minutes to stitch. You can stitch during a Little League game, a visit to the doctor, or while sitting on a friend's porch on a fresh spring day. You can even enjoy a cup of tea while you appliqué. Why not invite a few friends over and enjoy stitching while you visit?

I have used the techniques in this book to teach many appliqué students successful appliqué skills. Freezer-paper pieces ensure accuracy and success with fabric pieces. Plastic templates help make multiple pieces in a quilt look consistent. Cardboard templates made from photo-album pages are accurate and durable. It's not a secret! You, too, can stitch smooth curves, pointy points, and perfectly round circles. As you learn more about appliqué, you will discover many other techniques and tricks to make it easier and even more fun. Listen to other stitchers and teachers. Some techniques work better for different people and in different situations. Try them all. Then go home and use the ones *you* like the best!

I love painting pictures with fabrics in an appliqué quilt and I know you will too. I hope that the designs and techniques in this book inspire you to make your first appliqué quilt—and many more to follow. Happy stitching!

Introduction

Have you always admired appliqué quilts, but weren't sure if you were ready to make one? This appliqué book was written just for you! It will give you a great start and help to build your confidence. You'll learn how to stitch straight edges, curves, points, and circles. The little appliqué quilt projects included in this book are colorful and fun, and they are designed especially for the beginner.

• The quilts require a minimum number of fabrics so you need only make a few decisions as you plan and purchase supplies.

• The pattern shapes are smooth, with just a few inside and outside points to encourage you to develop your stitching skills.

• Most of the designs are applied to the background square in single layers, so it's easy to follow the stitching sequence.

• All of the appliqué designs are for use on 6" squares of background fabric.

Included here are three "Techniques for Sure Success" for preparing appliqué pieces. They are all fun, easy, and, of course, successful!

As you read, you'll see some symbols alongside the text. Here is what they mean:

Tip boxes include tricks of the trade and handy hints that will make a particular process or technique a bit easier. Read these right away!

Alert boxes will let you know when you really need to be careful. Your guardian angel will alert you so you don't make a common mistake.

Down the Road boxes contain information that will come in handy on future projects, after you have more quiltmaking experience. You don't need this information right away, though, so feel free to save the Down the Road ideas until you are ready to explore a bit more.

Read through the entire book before you start to appliqué. The main focus of this book is appliqué techniques. The directions in this book will gently guide you through the process of stitching a hand-appliquéd pillow, table runner, or wall quilt. There are books listed at the end that will help you with the process of quilting and finishing.

So—it's time to get out your favorite basket and fill it with needles and pins and your favorite small scissors. Choose some colorful fabrics. And get ready to appliqué!

Appliqué Terms

Appliqué: A method of sewing pieces of fabric on top of a larger background fabric piece to create a colorful design.

Appliqué Stitch: An almost invisible, small stitch used to attach appliqué fabric to the background fabric.

Background Fabric: A large piece of fabric, usually square, to which appliqué shapes are stitched.

Basting: Temporarily holding fabric in place by stitching, pinning, or gluing.

Bias Grain: The fabric grain that runs at a 45-degree angle to the lengthwise and crosswise threads in the fabric. Fabric has the greatest amount of stretch on the bias grain.

Freezer-Paper Appliqué: A method of preparing appliqué shapes using templates cut from freezer paper.

Fussy Cutting: Cutting an appliqué piece from a specific area of a fabric design, for example, leaves, flower petals, birds' wings.

Glue Basting: Using a dab of gluestick to temporarily hold fabric in place.

Hand Basting: Using needle, thread, and running stitches to temporarily hold fabric in place.

Layered Appliqué: Appliqué pieces that cover parts of other appliqué pieces.

Needle-Turn Appliqué: A method of turning the seam allowance under the appliqué pieces as you sew them to the background fabric, rather than turning them under before stitching them in place.

Pin Basting: Using pins to temporarily hold fabric in place.

Seam Allowance: The extra fabric outside the finished appliqué shape. The standard appliqué seam allowance is ¼" on all sides of an appliqué piece. Sometimes the directions may say "skimpy" or "generous" ¼" seam allowance. This means to make your seam allowance just a little narrower or wider than ¼".

Straight Grain: The straight threads that run the length (lengthwise grain) and width (crosswise grain) of the fabric.

Template: An appliqué shape cut from plastic or cardboard and used as a pattern for tracing a design onto fabric or paper. Appliqué templates are made the finished size of the shape and do not include seam allowances.

Fabric Selection

I hope you have a wonderful quilt shop nearby. Most quilt shops have a fabulous selection of fabrics perfect for appliqué projects. Take this book with you the next time you visit. The quilters there will be glad to help you choose just the right fabrics for your project.

Fabrics made of 100% cotton are easier to appliqué than those made of synthetic fibers, which tend to fray more than cotton and are often slippery. Sometimes, however, the "perfect" fabric contains synthetic fibers, and it's worth a little extra care to use it in your design. Contemporary appliqué artists often use a variety of fabrics, including lamé and satin, but I don't recommend this approach for beginners.

When you choose fabrics for appliqué projects, you need fabrics for two purposes: the background fabric and the appliqué fabrics.

Background Fabrics

Appliqué background fabrics are usually light, solid colors or small prints that complement the appliqué design. Avoid choosing prints or stripes that are too bold; they may make it difficult to see the appliquéd design.

White background fabrics add brightness and clarity to your appliqués, while off-white backgrounds enhance the richness of colors. White-on-white or off-white prints are lovely choices for stitchers who prefer a subtle print rather than a solid background.

Sometimes it is very appropriate to choose a special print for your design. The "water" fabric in the quilt, "School's Out," on page 50 is the perfect background for a school of fantasy fish.

Appliqué Fabrics

Choose fabrics for your appliqué pieces that are appropriate for the design. Sometimes the appliqué design will "talk to you." If there are leaves, it will tell you to make them green; if there are hearts, it will speak to you of red or pink. Think about the designs you are "painting with fabric." Shop for colors and fabric prints that you think go with the designs.

To determine a color palette for your quilt, it's fun to first choose a multicolored fabric that you love. Use the colors in this "inspiration" fabric as the color scheme in your quilt. Sometimes fabrics have little color dots along the selvage. Match these dots with coordinating fabrics for the appliqué pieces. Use the "inspiration" fabric for appliqué pieces, borders to frame your design, or on the back of the quilt.

> Solid fabrics may seem like good choices for appliqués, but print fabrics are a little more exciting and help conceal your stitches on the appliqué edges!

Fabric designs printed with two tones of the same color, such as dark green leaves printed over a slightly lighter green, appear to be solid colors but have a wonderful, subtle texture. Sometimes the designs of printed fabrics create lines that can be cut into leaf shapes or flower petals with realistic-looking veins. Fabrics printed with leaves and flowers are wonderful to use in appliqué because you can cut out whole flowers, individual petals, or leaves to give a realistic look to your appliqués. Use basket-weave prints for baskets, or wood-grain prints for stems. "Nature prints" provide opportunities to represent water and sky, or even bird feathers.

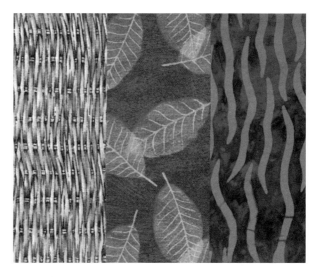

Fabrics printed with splashes of color provide wonderful appliqué pieces. The changes in color add depth and dimension to your designs. For example, you could cut a bird from a dark area of the fabric, and its wing from a lighter area for added realism.

Be brave! Try using the right and wrong sides of the same fabric to add shading to a design. The flower pots in "Dutch Treat" on page 54 were made with the right side for the rim and the wrong side for the bottom of the pots. It may seem unusual to use the wrong side, but wonderful effects often result.

Large-scale prints may seem inappropriate for appliqué, but a small piece cut from a specific area may make the perfect flower petal or bird's wing. This is sometimes called "fussy cutting."

Preview the fabrics for appliqué pieces by making a "window" template. Trace the pattern piece onto plain white paper. Cut out the shape, creating a hole, or window. Place the window over the fabric to "preview" the appliqué piece. Move the window around on the fabric surface to find just the right area to create the desired effect. Sometimes this can be a very subtle effect, but taking the time for this kind of planning can elevate your work from nice to very special.

Fabric Grain

Fabric is made of lengthwise threads that run along the length of the fabric, interwoven with crosswise threads that run across the fabric width from selvage to selvage. Therefore, fabric has two straight grain lines: lengthwise grain and crosswise grain. Fabric also has bias grain; it runs at a 45-degree angle to the lengthwise and crosswise grains. It has lots of stretch.

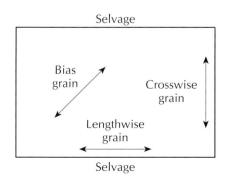

Whenever you cut a background square, border, or sashing strips for a quilt, they should be cut on the straight grain. This will keep your quilt straight and flat. When you cut appliqué pieces, it is usually not necessary to worry about the fabric grain. There are some shapes that behave better if they are placed on the bias of the fabric. For example, the inside point at the top of a heart will not fray if the heart is cut on the bias.

Curved seam allowances on leaves will turn under easily if the leaves are cut on the bias.

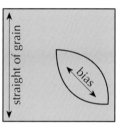

If you have a very special fabric, and you're using a window template to fussy-cut a piece, don't worry about grain line. Cut the shape to take best advantage of the fabric design and enjoy the way the fabric and appliqué design work together.

Fabric Paste-Ups

How can you be sure you've chosen the right fabrics? Make a color paste-up of your colors for one block before you start to cut and stitch the blocks. Trace your pattern onto a sheet of paper, cut the appliqué shapes out of your fabrics, then glue them to the design in the appropriate positions. Make several paste-ups to "audition" different fabrics to find the right one. Auditioning helps you make decisions about the color arrangements before you begin stitching. Use the final paste-up as a placement guide while you stitch.

Fabric Preparation

Most appliqué stitchers prewash their fabrics to preshrink them, remove sizing, and test for colorfastness. Wash dark and light colors separately. Sometimes it is necessary to wash and rinse dark-colored fabrics several times to remove excess dye. Dark reds, purples, and some greens have a reputation for "bleeding"—something you definitely don't want to happen in *your* quilt! It's important to check fabrics for bleeding because you will be appliquéing fabrics onto light background fabrics.

To test a dark fabric for colorfastness, cut a small piece, get it wet, and place it on a scrap of background fabric. Let the pieces dry together.

If color shows up on the background fabric, wash and test the fabric again—or choose a different fabric. Take the time to prewash your fabrics. This ensures that your finished quilt will not shrink and that the colors won't bleed onto each other when the quilt is laundered.

Orvus paste is a good soap to use for washing your fabrics. It is available in most quilt shops in a little white jar marked "Quilt Soap." It is gentle and washes out easily.

Press fabrics to remove wrinkles so you can accurately cut the appliqué and background pieces. Some quilters apply spray starch or sizing to help give fabrics extra body, making them easier to handle.

Tools and Supplies

Appliqué stitchers travel lightly! You will need a small tote bag or basket to keep your work and your favorite tools handy.

Needles: The most important consideration when choosing a needle is the size. A sharp, fine needle glides easily through the edges of appliqué pieces, creating small invisible stitches. In needle language, the higher the number, the finer the needle. Try sizes 10–12 for the best results.

The type of needle used for hand appliqué is a personal choice. Some appliqué stitchers use short quilting needles called "betweens" because they feel closer to their stitches. The "official" appliqué needles are longer and they are called "sharps." An even longer needle called a "straw" or "milliner's" works well for "needle-turning" the appliqué edges as you stitch it to the background. Try different needles to find the one most comfortable for you.

Between

Sharp

Milliner's

Thread: Appliqué thread should match the color of the appliqué pieces, *not* the background fabric. Several shades of thread are required for designs with different-colored pieces. If it is not possible to match the color exactly, choose thread that is a little darker than the fabric. For appliqué fabrics that are printed with many colors, choose a thread that blends with the predominant color. Sometimes a neutral brown or gray blends perfectly.

All-cotton thread works well for hand stitching. It blends invisibly into the edges of all-cotton appliqués. If you can't find all-cotton thread, use cotton-covered polyester. Size 50 thread is all-purpose sewing thread and can be found in all sewing stores. Size 60 is a finer thread and will improve the invisibility of your stitches.

Needle Threader: If a needle is difficult to thread, use a needle threader to insert the thread through the eye of the needle.

Pins: Use small straight pins to pin-baste appliqué pieces to the background fabric. My favorites are ¾"-long pins because they do not get in the way of the thread as you stitch.

Scissors: A good, sharp pair of little scissors is often a stitcher's most prized possession; one is essential for clipping threads, clipping inside points, and trimming appliqué pieces. You will also need a pair of "paper" scissors to cut paper, cardboard, or plastic templates.

Thimble: Use a thimble to protect your finger as you push the needle through your fabric. If you can't get used to a metal thimble, try a soft thimble made out of leather.

Rulers: All of the appliqué designs in this book are designed for 6" finished squares. Use a 9½"-square (or larger) acrylic ruler to mark and cut the background fabric squares for your projects. Look for a 6½"-square ruler for trimming the blocks to the perfect size after appliquéing.

Gluestick: Water-soluble gluestick is handy for basting seam allowances and for basting appliqué pieces in position on the background fabric.

Fabric Markers: Choose from a variety of fabric markers to trace appliqué designs onto the background fabric. Use silver marking pencils, water-erasable pens, or fine-lead mechanical pencils for light fabrics. For dark fabrics, use sharp chalk pencils in white or yellow. It is always wise to test markers on a scrap of fabric to make sure they can be easily removed.

Template Plastic and Permanent Markers: Trace the designs onto the template plastic to make patterns for the appliqué designs. Use a fine-tip permanent marking pen.

Plastic Circle Stencil: Found in most office- and art-supply stores, this handy stencil contains circles in different sizes. Use it to draw perfect circles.

Freezer Paper: Available at most grocery stores and quilt shops, freezer paper has a shiny plastic coating on one side. The coated side softens and sticks to fabric when you apply a dry, warm iron to the uncoated side. Use it to make templates for appliqués.

Iron: Use an iron to attach freezer-paper templates to your fabric and for pressing your finished blocks. (Most quilters I know do not iron shirts! They're too busy stitching.)

Tape: Use Scotch Removable Magic Tape to tape your fabric to your pattern while you trace the design onto your background fabric. It will not rip the paper or fray your fabric.

Tweezers: A small pair of tweezers makes it easy to remove freezer paper after you have appliquéd a piece to the background.

Stiletto: This pointed tool will help you hold your fabric shapes in place on the work surface as you prepare them with glue or an iron.

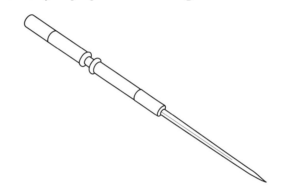

Plastic Bags: What did we do before zip-top bags were invented? They're super for keeping your appliqué pieces organized and your work-in-progress clean.

Pillow: Place a 12"- to 14"-square pillow in your lap under your work. It provides a nice pincushion, a comfortable place to rest your hands, and helps improve your posture as you stitch.

Your Favorite Chair and Lamp: You will find that you are more comfortable and can make smaller stitches if you sit in your favorite chair with the light from a favorite lamp over your shoulder aimed at your work.

Sewing Machine: You don't need a sewing machine to do hand appliqué! Let your machine rest while you enjoy stitching the pieces in place. Send it out for a well-deserved cleaning! It will come in handy when you sew the quilt top together.

2ND EDITION

Start Quilting

with
Alex Anderson

Six Projects for First-Time Quilters

C&T PUBLISHING